E5 Life STRATEGIES, INC.

PRESENTS

_____

Adapted from Dr. Don Lichi, PTH-P 936 Crisis Counseling, Assemblies of God Theological Seminary. Used with Permission.

Scripture quotations are from the ESV®Bible (The Holy Bible, English Standard Version®), copyright© 2001 by Crossway Bibles, a publishing ministry of Good News Publishers. Used by permission. All rights reserved.

Cover Image: Angel Lutcher
Cover Design: Katie Zeliger, Meraki Press
Layout: Katie Zeliger and Wyeth Doty, Meraki Press

E5 Life Strategies, Inc.,
PO Box 1095,
Maricopa, AZ 85139
www.e5lifestrategies.com

ISBN: 979-8-9885850-3-9

Printed in the United States of America

First Printing, November 2023

TABLE OF CONTENTS

LAYER one

LAYER two

LAYER three

LAYER ONE
self-story review

LAYER TWO
talents, abilities and educational experiences

LAYER THREE
Prophetic Perspective

LAYER ONE

Self-Story Review

IN A
shallow world
CHOOSE
— to be —
deep

Section One

Self-Story Review

Self-story review

Section one

how do I see myself

Strengths...

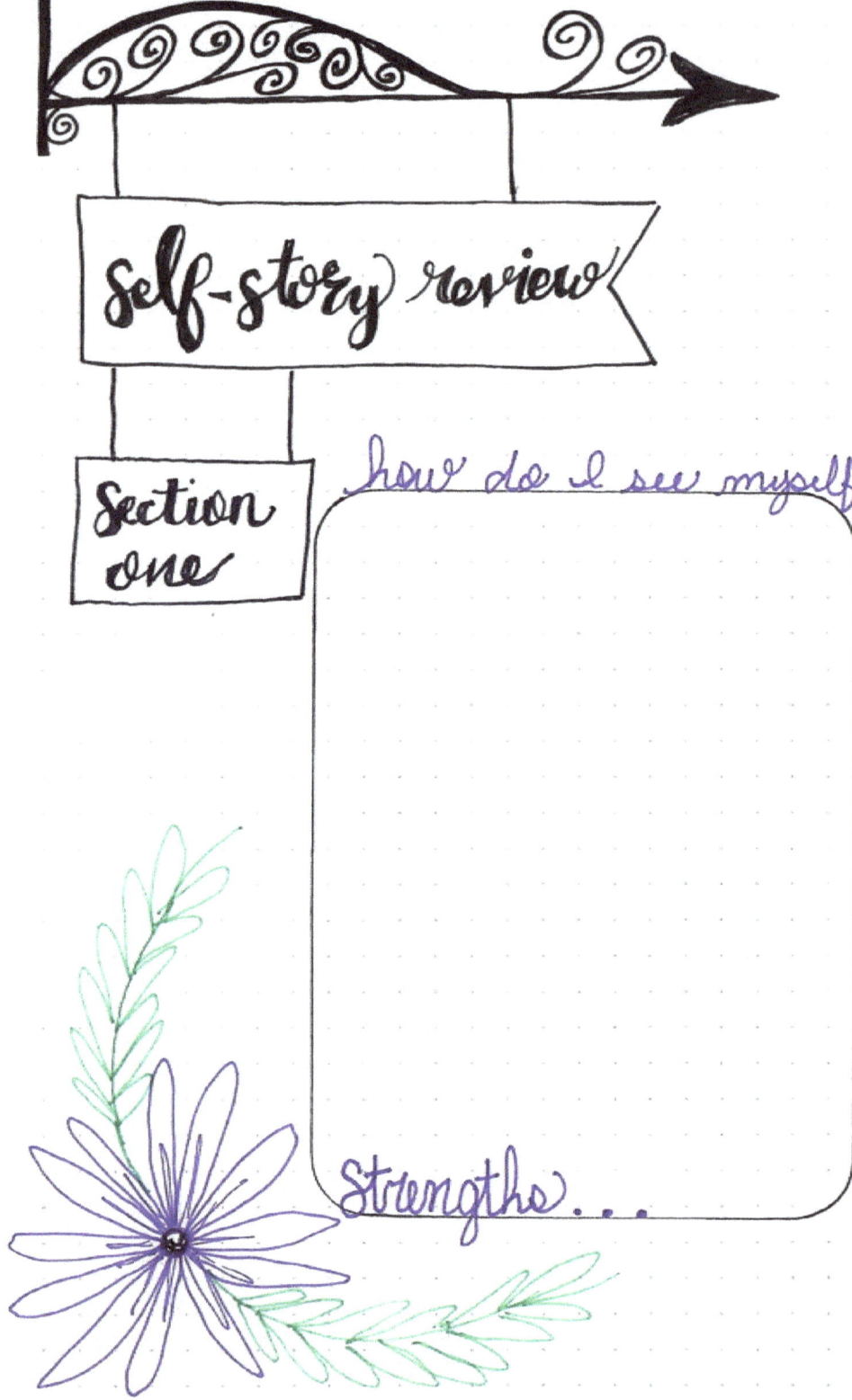

Weaknesses...

talents...

abilities ...

LIES
I believe about myself

- [ ]
- [ ]
- [ ]
- [ ]
- [ ]
- [ ]
- [ ]
- [ ]
- [ ]
- [ ]
- [ ]

TRUTH
what does God say

Reflection ...

what are
some obstacles
that inhibit
your growth?

behaviors
or traits
that
summarizes
you as a
person

...reflection

Your View of Others

Do you perceive others as basically trustworthy and good, self-serving and egocentric, or something in-between?

Around people are you usually at ease, tense or on guard?

Your View of others

When you think of individuals as a whole, what comes to mind

... reflections

your view of life

Does the world seem like a fair, impartial, or unfair place to you?

Do you see yourself as not having control, or having control in relation to the world about you?

Do you view the world as being a comfortable or some what uncomfortable place as you move about from day to day?

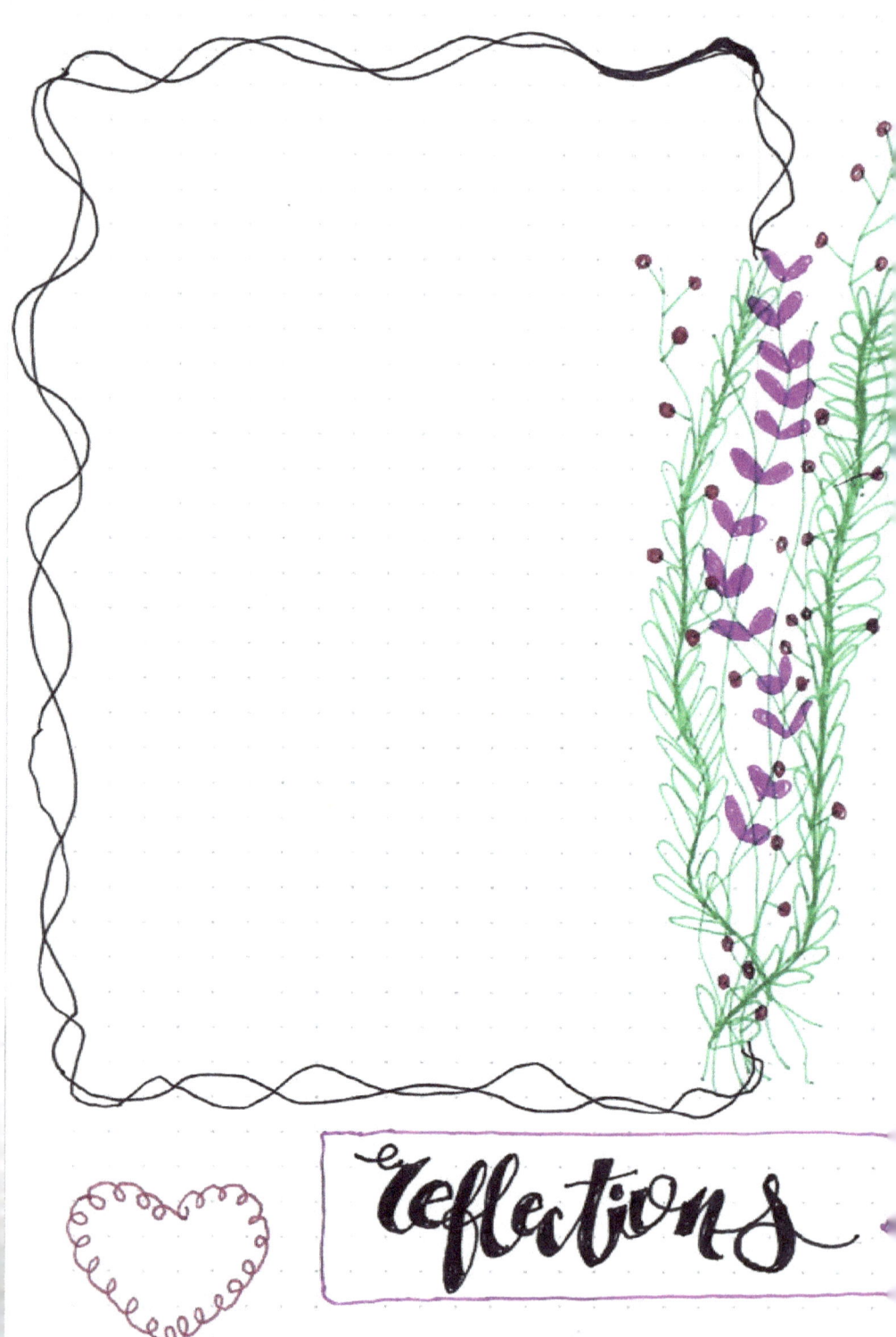

reflections

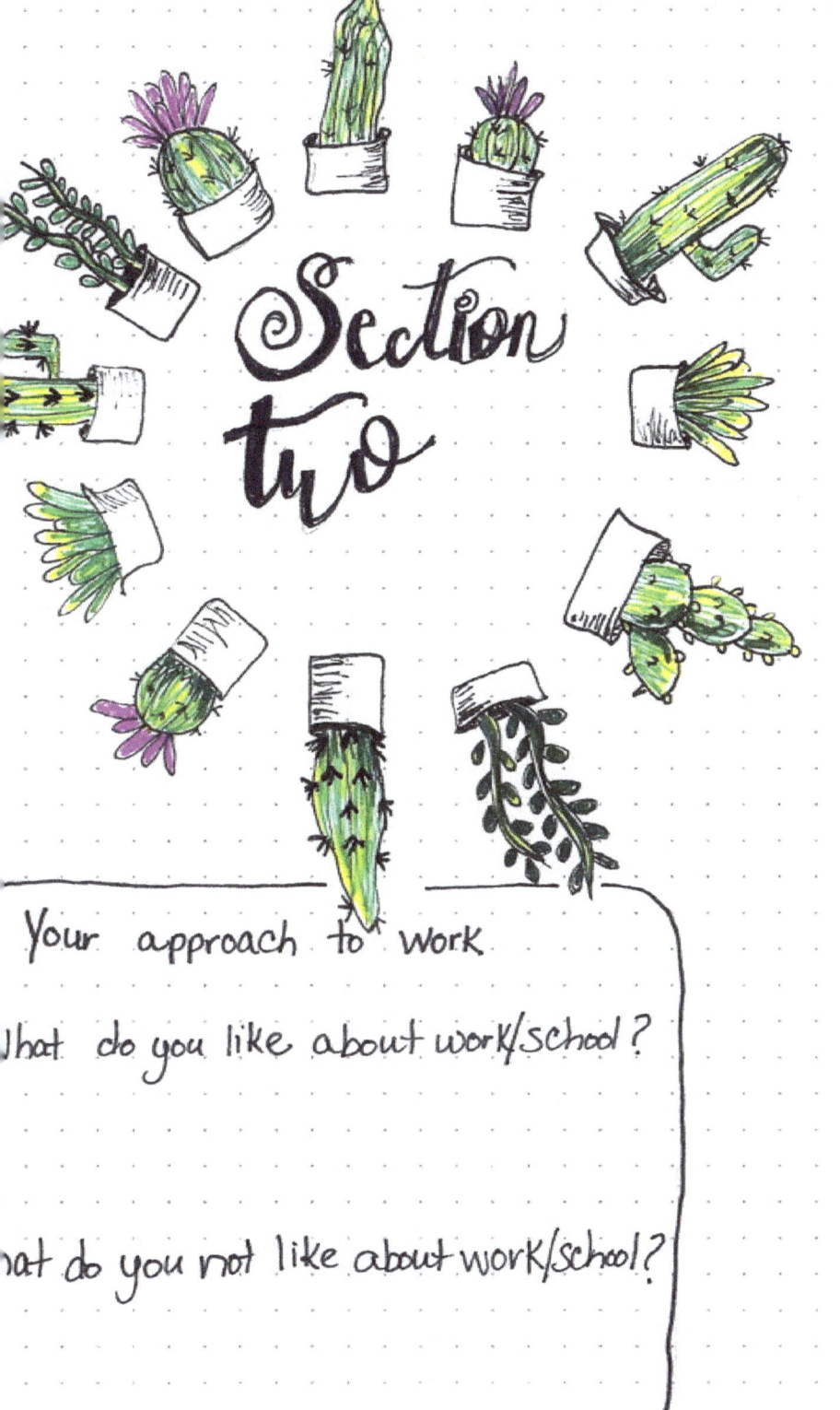

Section two

Your approach to work

What do you like about work/school?

What do you not like about work/school?

work...

hat is your feelings
onward your work/school
perience as a whole?

Social
Relationships

how do you feel when
you interact with
others socially?

reflections.....

reflections

Social Relationships

Are you someone who iniates, follows,or someone who does both in your inter-personal relationships?

Social
Relationships

how would you characterize
  yourself in the relationship
you have?

reflections

your approach to
Love relati...

How do you
feel about
the intimate relations in
which you now are
involved or have
been involved?

ships

How do you view your
love relationships

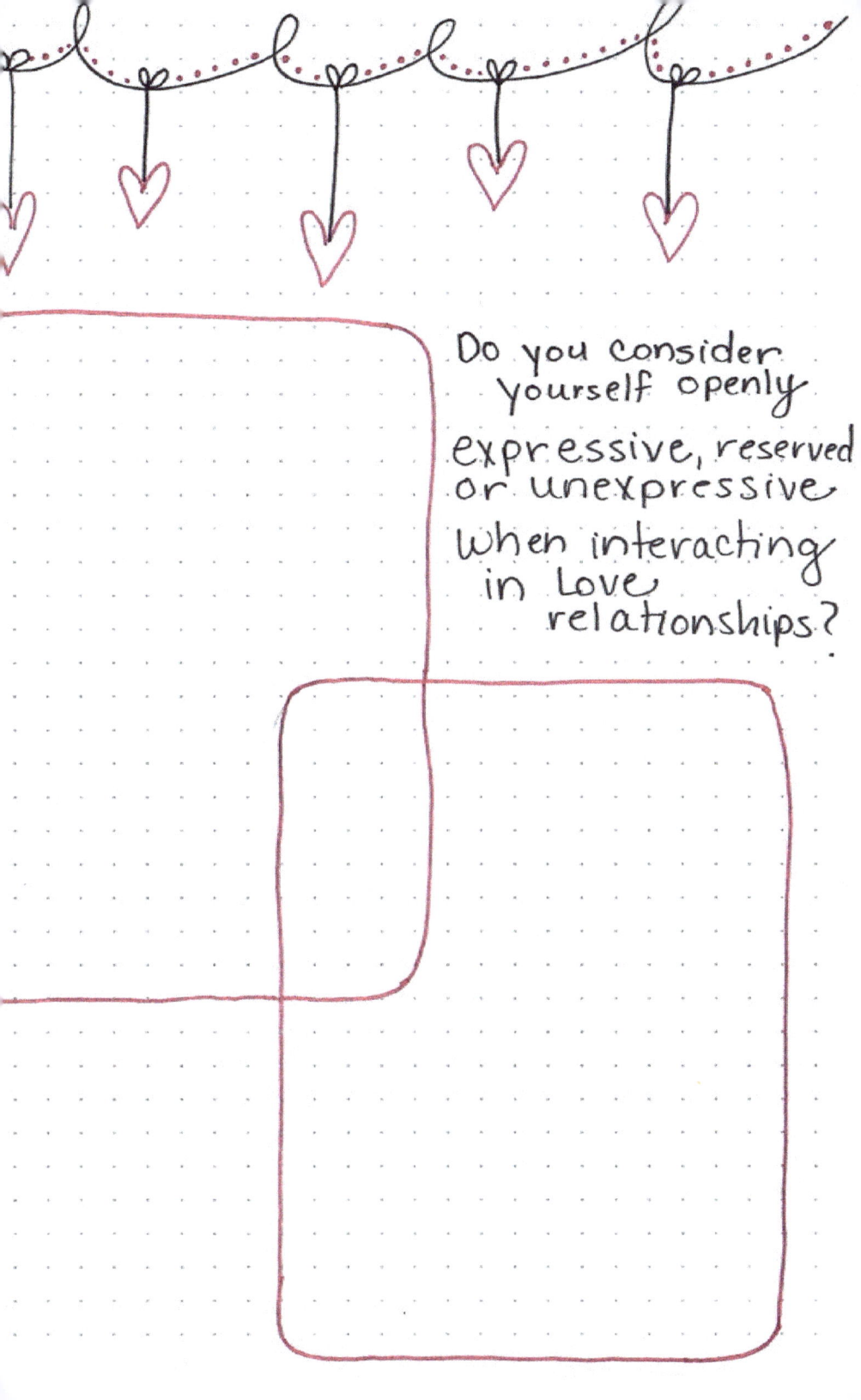

Do you consider yourself openly expressive, reserved or unexpressive when interacting in love relationships?

HOW would you describe yourself in past or current relationships?

Reflections

section three

family relationships

escription of your

FATHER

and your relationship
with him

Is he loving? caring? concerned?
distant? or aloof?

Father

does he s
to have t
for you? or
he usually
busy?

Does others
get more of
his attention
than you

Father

How
does
your
father
seem to
function
in the world
about
him?

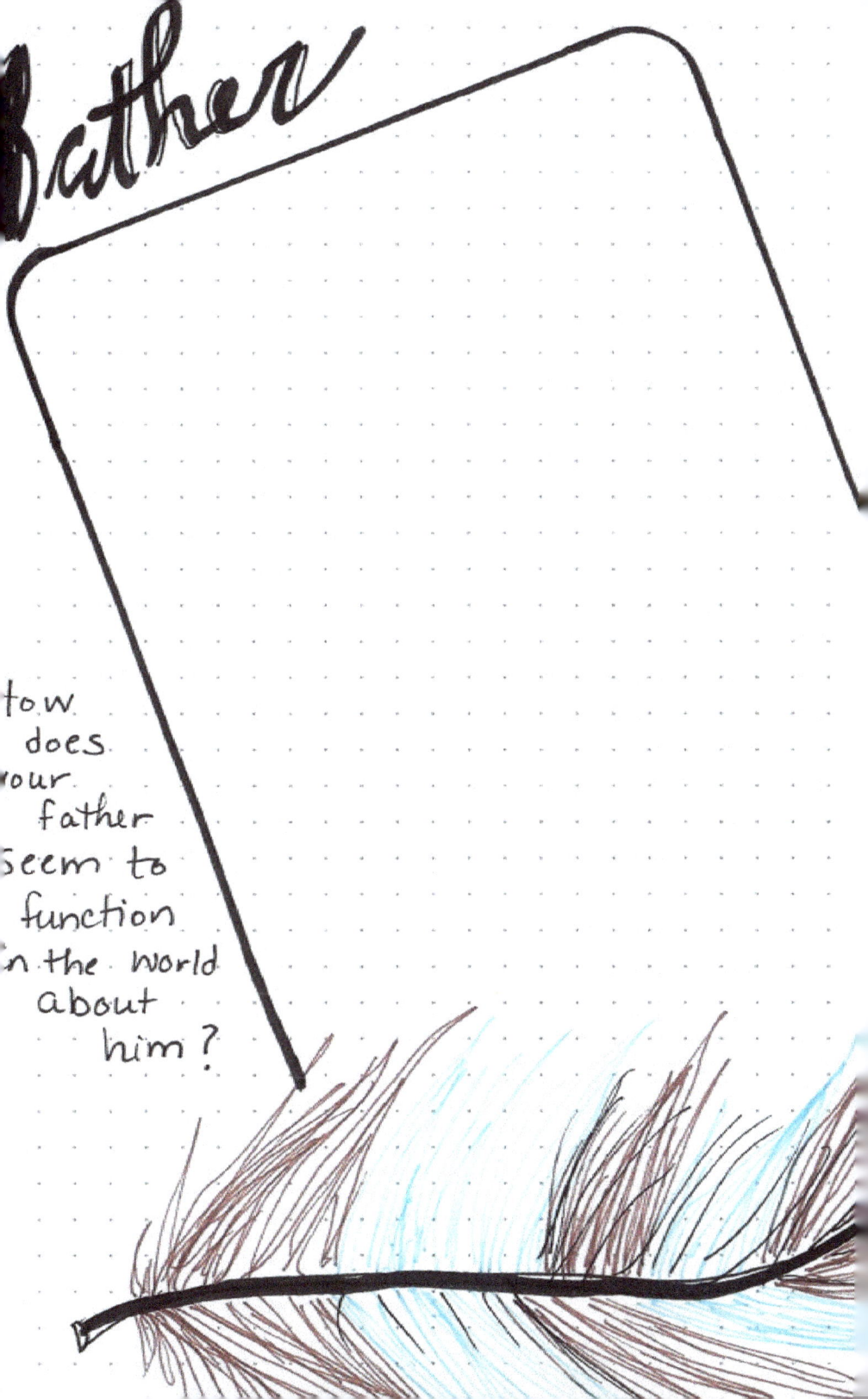

reflections

Mother

- does your mother tend to be
  dominant?
  submissive?
  cooperative?

- how does she act
  and interact
  with you?

- how does she approach
  and cope
  with life?

Mother

describe how you percive your mother, and how you view your relationship with her.

Mother♡

Mother

siblings....

what is your brother or sisters like

siblings

what kind of relationship do you have
with your siblings
            indicate their ages
    as you refer to them

siblings

what sibling do you tend to get along with, or not get along with? and why?

Siblings

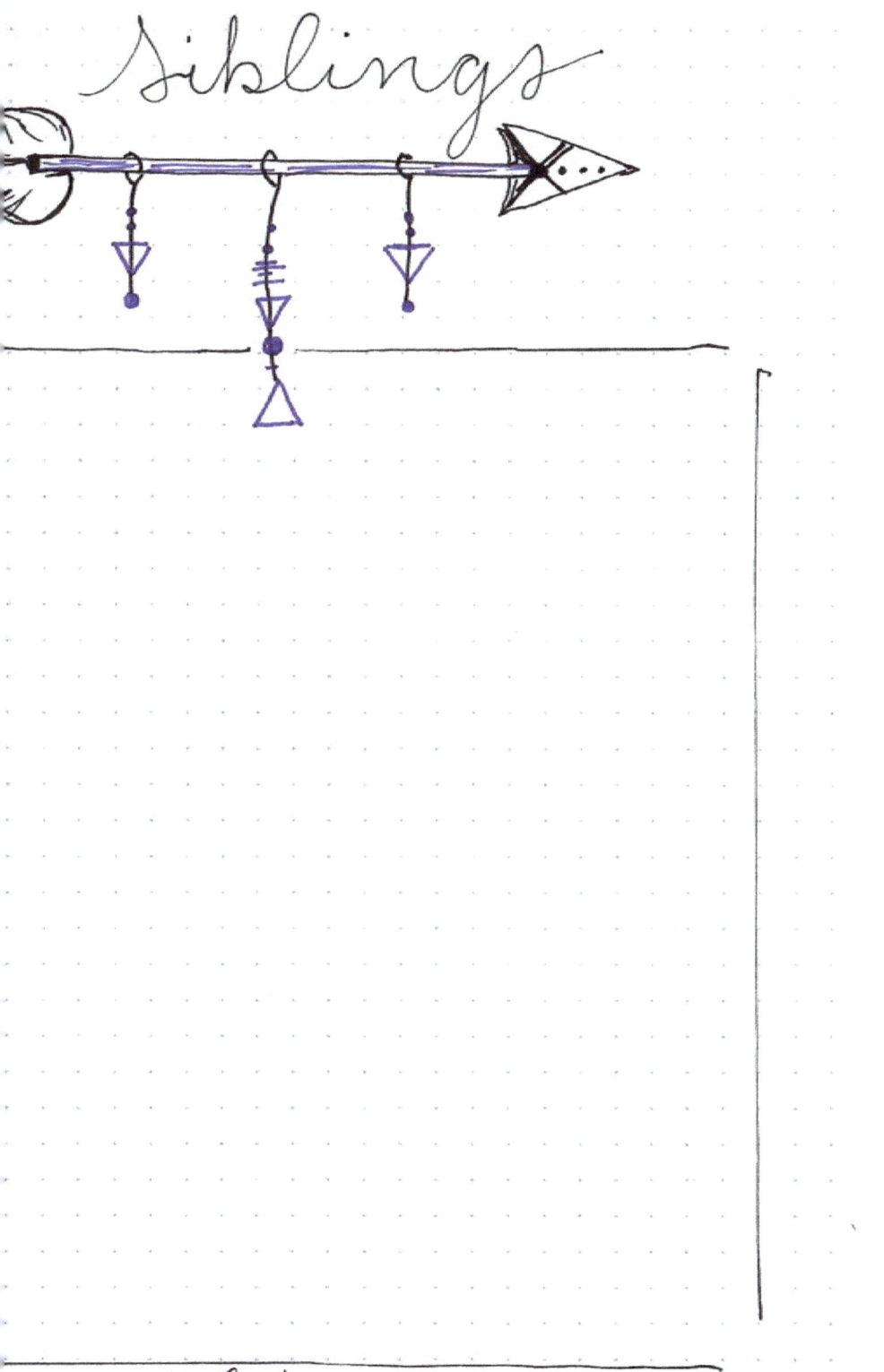

t has life been like growing
up with your siblings?

siblings

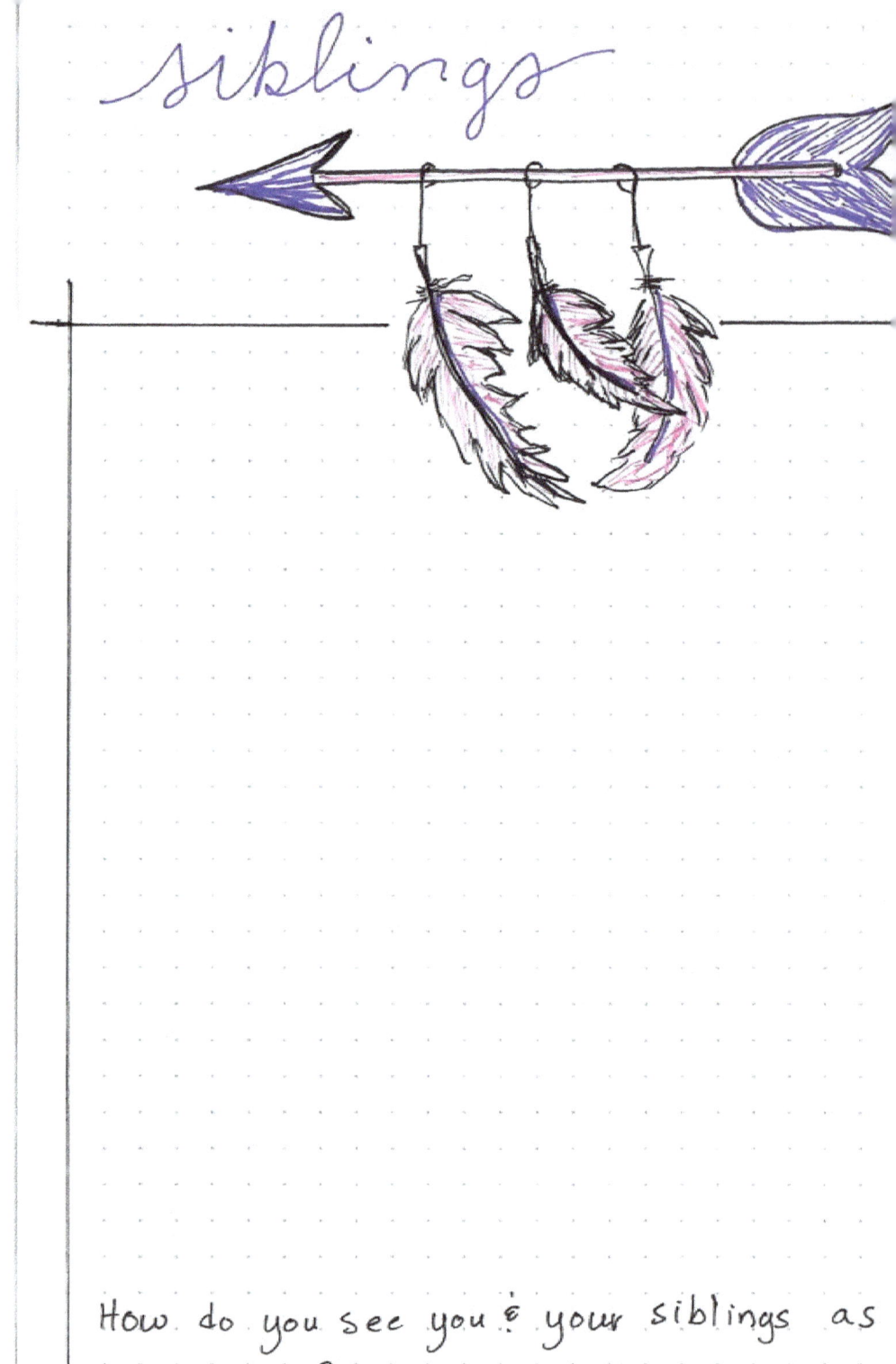

How do you see you & your siblings as functioning collectively

reflections

until
we are in
Christ
we are LOST
and
until Christ is in
us we are
LIMITED

LAYER TWO

talents, abilities and
educational experiences

EDUCATION

training and educational experiences that you have received?

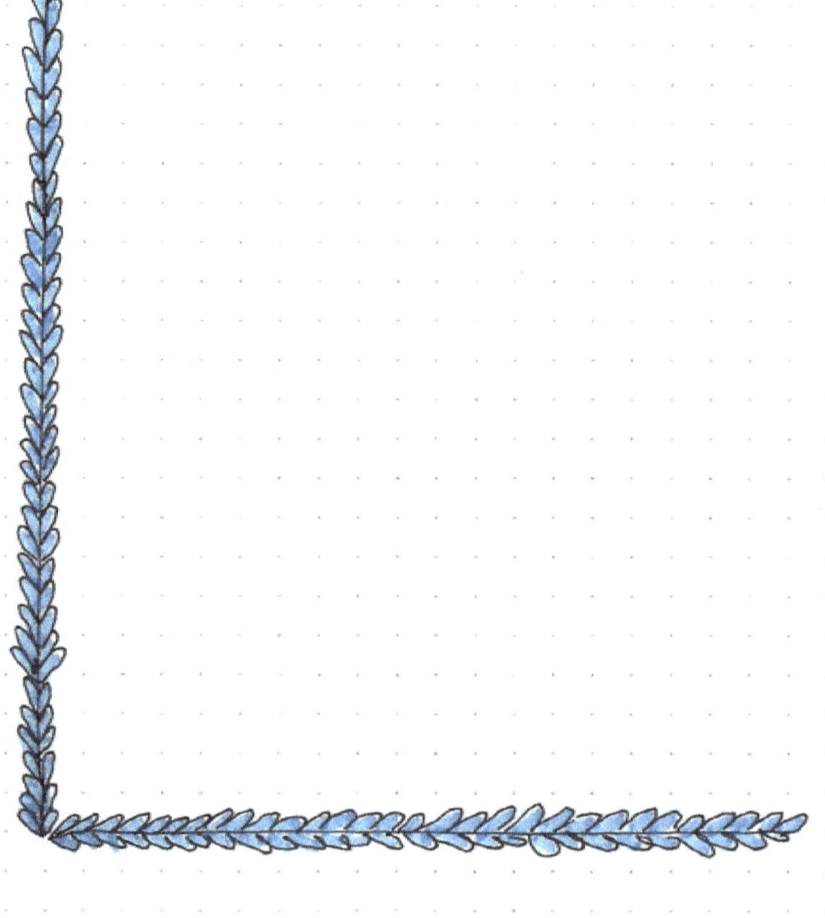

What angers you?

What makes you CRY?

what have you mastered?

what gives you hope?

what do you look forward to?

what great vision do you have for your future?

how about for the future of others?

HOPE.

what gives you
hope?

forward

what do you look forward to?

FUTURE vision

what great vision do you have for your future?

Others future VISION

What great vision do you have for the future of others?

As a child
What did you
want to be
when you grew up?

IF you had all the time and money the world what would you do?

WHAT would blow your mind?

list 40 things that would blow your mind if they happened.

reflections

PLATFORM

never trust someone who says they want to see the world change, but can't affect change in their own neighborhood.

What platform do you have for self-expression? What foundation can you build onto begin affecting the kind of change you would like to see?

CHANGE

what big change would you like to see before you die?

what would be different about the WORLD because you lived?

if you had one day left, how would you spend it?

Jesus came to this earth to forgive our sin, free us from its power, And fill us with His Spirit. So we could live in the fullness of His presence.

Dr. Shelly Hogan
E5 life Strategies Inc.

LAYER THREE
prophetic perspective

Any pertinent recent revelation you have gained on particular scripture passages.

reflections

PROPHETIC

hat are some prophetic words
that have been spoken
over you by others

PROPHETIC

PROPHETIC

- [ ]
- [ ]
- [ ]
- [ ]
- [ ]
- [ ]
- [ ]
- [ ]
- [ ]
- [ ]
- [ ]
- [ ]
- [ ]
- [ ]
- [ ]

prophecies

sensings
&
promptings
that you have felt from the Lord

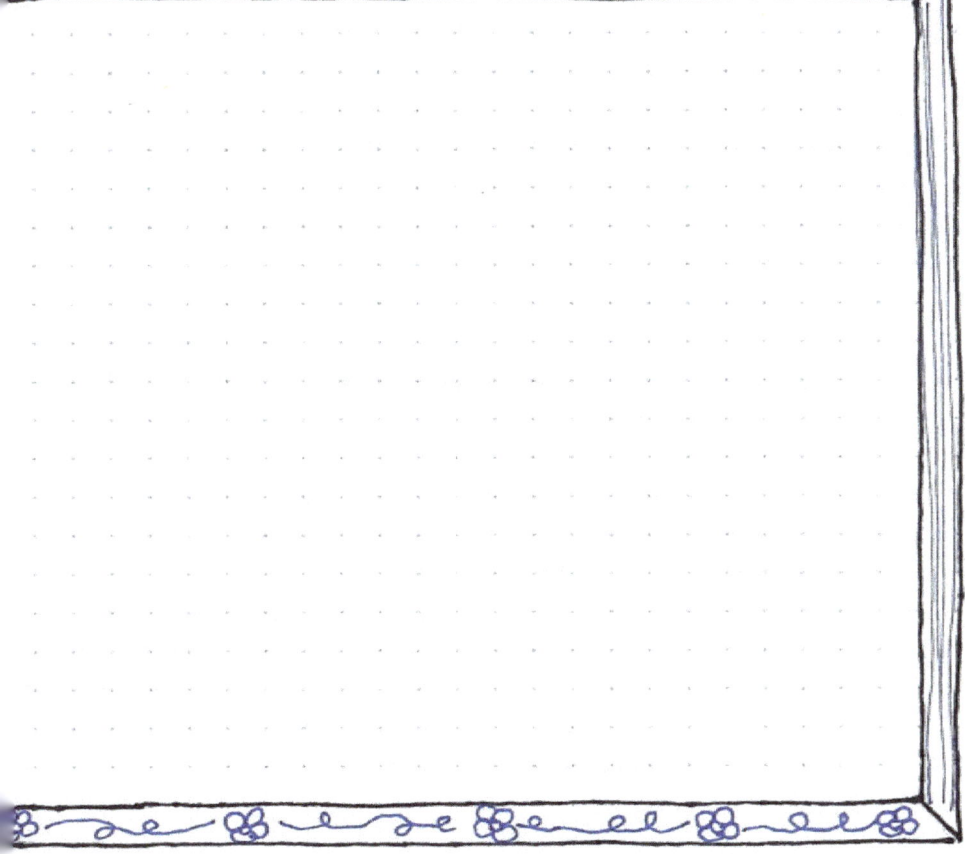

NEVER

let your fears

SPEAK LOUDER

than your

FAITH

Dreams
*that stay with you
after you awaken*

dreams

that stay with you after
you awaken

Significant Encounters

prayers

Significant Encounters

Church Services

Significant Encounters

special religious events

reflections

reflections

LAYERED LIFE MAP

Psalms 139:14 declares, "I praise you, for I am fearfully and wonderfully made. Wonderful are your works; my soul knows it very well." Each person is a unique and wonderful expression of God on the earth. One definition of wonderful is "of a sort that causes wonder; amazing; astonishing."

You are an amazing and inspiring work of God! Sadly, we are often unaware of just how wonderful we are and many people struggle with feelings of inadequacy and aimlessness. The layered life map invites you to the second greatest discovery you can make after accepting Christ as your Lord and Savior: your unique design, purpose, and passion. This journey is for those intentional on walking into next levels of intimacy with God and fruitfulness in serving. Proverbs 25:2 "It is the glory of God to conceal things, but the glory of kings is to search things out." Take time to work through each layer and get ready for great discovery!

Layer 1: Self-Story Review
Fill out the Self-administered Lifestyle Analysis (SALSA) provided with this form.

Layer 2: Talents, abilities, and educational experience
Write a brief paragraph detailing the following:
1. Specific training and educational experiences that you have received.
2. Encounters, events, and experiences that you tend to gravitate toward. What do you like to do?
3. Answer these 10 vision catching questions:
A. *What angers you?* Every superhero needs a bad guy. Without one, the super hero has nothing to fight against. Are there specific things that evoke a compassionate anger in you?
B. *What makes you cry?* Think about the last several instances that caused you to cry. Movies are fair game too. Stories of triumph through trials.

---

1 www.dictionary.com/browse/wonderful Accessed March 26, 2018.

C. *What have you mastered?* Are there tasks, skills, or opportunities that you have simply mastered and can do without thinking? These low-friction activities might give you a clue to ways you can continue pursuing your voice. We learn through action, observation, then correction.

D. *What gives you hope?* What do you look forward to? What great vision do you have for your future and the future of others? Hope is a powerful motivator, and can give you a clue to the ways in which you may be able to
compel others to act.

E. *As a child, what did you want to be when you grew up?* We often forget the earliest clues to our voice as we are burdened with the expectations of
peers, teachers, parents, and eventually the marketplace. Consider those early days of wonder.

F. *If you had all the time and money in the world what would you do?* It's astounding how few people have asked themselves this question, and how few people can arrive at an answer when they do. We believe that a lack of resources is the obstacle to our happiness and fulfillment, but for many of us the limitation has nothing to do with a lack of time or money. The limitation is our fear of falling short of our own self perception.

G. *What would blow your mind?* Take about an hour to list 40 things that would blow your mind if they happened. You'll get to about 15 before you find it difficult. Keep going, including relational things, business things, travel, ambitions, hopes, etc. Some things will never happen. Nevertheless, it's a great way to *identify patterns in your motivation.*

H. *What platform do you own?* No need to start over. Build from where you are. What platform do you already have for self-expression? What foundation can you build on to begin affecting the kind of change you'd like to see? Never trust someone who says they want to see the world change, but can't affect change in their own neighborhood.

I. *What change would you like to see in the world?* If you could identify a single *delta*—a big change you would like to see before you die—what would
it be? What would be different about the world because you lived? Don't be afraid to think big, but be specific. You may not be the one to lead this change, but you may be able to play a significant role in it. (By the way... think relationships here too. The biggest change you and I have the capacity to make is in the lives of others).

J. *If you had one day left, how would you spend it?* If you knew that you would evaporate at midnight, how would you spend your last day on earth? What questions would you ask? Who would you spend time with? What work would you do? Again, this is an interesting way to begin identifying patterns within your passions, skills, and experiences.

4. Ask 2 or 3 trusted friends who know you well to look over your answers and give their input on your answers. Ask them to honestly share their insight about you.

5. Take the spiritual gifts test at https://spiritualgiftstest.com/spiritual-gifts test-adult-version/

Layer 3: Prophetic perspective

Habakkuk 2: 2-3 "And the Lord answered me: 'Write the vision; make it plain on tablets, so he may run who reads it. For still the vision awaits its appointed time; it hastens to the end—it will not lie. If it seems lost, wait for it; it will surely come; it will not delay." God speaks to us through His Word, through dreams, and through prophetic proclamations and insights. It is essential that we keep a journal record of these encounters to review, prayer over, and proclaim over our lives. These words will bear witness to and come in alignment with our gifts, talents, dreams, and goals and help to bring affirmation and clarity.

Review and describe the following:
1. Any pertinent recent revelation you have gained on particular scripture passages.
2. Prophetic words that have been spoken over to you by others.
3. Sensings and promptings that you have felt from the Lord.
4. Dreams that stay with you after you awaken.
5. Significant encounters in times of prayer, church services, or special religious events.

Review of layers
Layer 1:

1. Our relationships with others tend to impact how we view God. Acknowledge if there are any relationships that have caused you to get a wrong view (in opposition to scripture) of God. Repent, forgive those who have hurt you, and ask God to heal your understanding and reveal Himself to you in powerful ways.
2. Review main events of your childhood and young adulthood. Recognize that negative events could have been used by the enemy to deter or destroy your destiny while positive events may hold clues to your God-given passions and purpose.
3. If you are feeling stuck in this area connect with E5 to schedule a consult or prayer session.

Layer 2:

1. What insights have you gained about yourself?
2. Ask God to give you a strategic plan to grow in your areas of gifts and passion. Is there a place in the local body you can serve in aligning with your heart? What training/educational pursuits do you need to engage in to go to the next level?

Layer 3:

1. What has God been speaking over you? Take time to thank Him for His guiding presence.
2. Schedule a personal retreat time of 24-48 hours. Disconnect from all electronics (phone, computer, etc.) and get alone with God. Take this time to pray, worship, journal, and encounter God. If it is hard for you to be alone, invite 1 or 2 like-minded friends who will encourage you in this process and participate with you. REMEMBER: This is not play time, or visit time. It is a time to intentionally pursue God and hear from heaven.
3. Intentionally look for the ways that God is active in your life and the activities that He is blessing. Purpose to partner with Him in this.
Share what God is showing you to trusted ministers and accountability partners. Ask them to pray with you as you are pursuing God's best. Each layer reveals information about your heart, passion, and experience as well as the activity of God in your life, church, and ministry. Look for the commonalities and through this process write out a "life statement," three or more sentences that define you: your heart, passion, and purpose.

Next steps:

Begin to seek the Lord on things that need to be pruned, perfected, and pursued (new training, etc.) to go to next levels.

Date _____

SELF-ADMINISTERED LIFE STYLE ANALYSIS

The *Self-Administered Life Style Analysis* (SALSA) is an instrument designed to elicit personal lifestyle information—that is, information about how you view a variety of different life areas. More specifically, you will be asked to indicate: (a) your view of yourself, others, and life in general; (b) your approach to the life tasks of work, social, and love relationships; (c) your descriptions of and relationships with parents and siblings; and (d) some of your early memories.

Instructions: Please respond to each of the following statements, providing the requested information. Write approximately one paragraph per statement for Sections I, II, and IV, and two paragraphs per statement for Section III. You will find three questions following every statement; these are meant merely to assist you in better understanding the statement should it seem vague. Therefore, feel free to use or not use the various questions, responding as you see fit.

SECTION I. *(Write 1 paragraph each for A, B and C)*
A. Your View of Self
Indicate briefly how you currently see yourself as an individual.
• What are some of the strengths you consider yourself to possess?
• What are some of the obstacles that inhibit your growth?
• What are some of the behaviors or traits that seem to summarize you as a person?

B. Your View of Others
Share the impressions or thoughts you have when you think of people in general.
• In other words, do you perceive others as basically trustworthy and good, self serving and egocentric, or something in-between?
• Around people, are you usually at ease, tense, or on guard?
• When you think of individuals as a whole, what comes to mind?

C. Your View of Life
Point out some of the basic assumptions, or general ideas, you have toward life.
• Does the world seem like a fair, impartial, or unfair place to you?
• Do you see yourself as having, or not having, control in relation to the world around you?
• Do you view the world as being a comfortable, or somewhat uncomfortable, place as you move about from day to day?

Adapted from Dr. Don Lichi, PTH-P 936 Crisis Counseling, Assemblies of God Theological [2] Seminary. Used with permission.

E5 Life Strategies, Inc., PO Box 1095, Maricopa, AZ 85139 Revised 3/26/18

SECTION II. *(Write 1 paragraph each for A, B and C)*

A. Your Approach to Work

State briefly how you feel toward the work/school in which you are involved.

• What do you like about work/school?

• What do you not like about work/school?

• What are your feelings toward your work/school experience as a whole?

B. Your Approach to Social Relationships

Provide some information as to how you approach your social relationships.

• How do you feel when you interact with others socially?

• Are you someone who initiates, follows, or some combination thereof, in your interpersonal relationships?

• How would you characterize yourself in the relationships you have?

C. Your Approach to Love Relationships

Indicate how you view your love relationships.

• How do you feel about the intimate relations in which you now are involved or have been involved?

• Do you consider yourself openly expressive, reserved, or unexpressive when interacting in love relationships?

• How would you describe yourself in past or current relations?

SECTION III. *(Write 2 paragraphs each for A, B and C)*

A. Description of your father, and your relationship with your father

Share a description of how you perceive your father (1 paragraph) and your relationship with him (one paragraph). (Please indicate his age)

• Is your father loving and caring, somewhat concerned, or distant and aloof?

• Does he seem to have time for you; is he usually busy, or do others seem to receive more attention from him than you?

• How does your father seem to function in the world about him?

B. Description of your mother, and your relationship with your mother

Share a brief description of how you perceive your mother (1 paragraph) and how you view your relationship with her (one paragraph). (Please indicate her age)

• Does your mother tend to be a dominant, submissive, or cooperative individual?

• How does she act toward, and interact with, you as a person?

• How would you characterize your mother as approaching and coping with life?

C. Description of your sibling(s), and your relationship with your sibling(s)
Describe what your brother(s) and sister(s) are like (1 paragraph). Describe what kind of relationships you have with your siblings (1 paragraph). (Indicate their ages as you refer to them.)
• Which siblings do you tend to get along with, or not get along with, and why?
• What has life been like in growing up with your brothers and/or sisters?
• How do you see you and your siblings as functioning collectively?

(Note: If you are an only child, describe your relationships with close peers or individuals who were like brothers and/or sisters to you.)

SECTION IV.
(Write 1 paragraph for each early recollection and/or development)
Early recollections (ERs) are early memories/crises that (a) occur before the age of eight; (b) can be visualized; and (c) are single, specific incidents. For example, an early recollection could run somewhat as follows: "Once, when I was about six, my father slipped up on my brother and me while we were playing. We were both surprised. Then, he told us he was going to take us to the circus later that afternoon. My brother and I were pleased."

This merely serves as an example to give you some idea of what an early recollection is —a specific, visualizable event occurring before the age of eight. Your memories can be expected to vary, and may include a variety of emotions such as ecstasy, contentment and/or depression. Please provide as many details as possible in each recollection, indicating your thoughts, feelings, and/or actions. After the memory has been written out, identify the age at which the recollection occurred and what aspect of it is most vivid for you. (Rev. 3.17).

Finally, include in your SALSA examples of personal, developmental, situational,
congregational or other types of "crises" in your life. How did you deal with the crisis then? How do you deal with the crisis now? What did you learn from the crisis experience? How have you managed to develop a "theodicy" that allows you to live more fully in the present despite the crisis?

MEET THE AUTHOR & ILLUSTRATOR

Dr. Shelly Hogan is a wife, mom to three grown children, nana to her wonderful grandchildren, and spiritual mama to many. While pastoring in Maricopa, AZ and completing her doctoral work at Assemblies of God Theological Seminary, Dr. Shelly had a radical encounter with the Lord that changed the trajectory of her life tremendously. She was "mugged by God" at a prayer retreat. This encounter was the impetus for founding E5 Life Strategies, Inc., a nonprofit Christian Ministry that exists to teach and build up the body of Christ by way of transformative retreat encounters, soul healing, empowering teaching, and sacred community development. Dr. Shelly has served as an associate pastor, lead pastor, college professor, and life coach. Dr. Shelly and her husband, Avnel, have been married for 39 years and love spending time with their adult children, their spouses, and their children. Dr. Shelly's passion is to see all people freed from past wounds and powerful in their walk with Christ.

Angel Lutcher is a wife, mom, grandma, entrepreneur, and a woman with many passions. She is a prayer warrior, world traveler, artist, and author. A Pennsylvania native, she has traveled for ministry all over the east coast, Arizona, and other parts of the world. Angel and her husband, Mark, have been settled in Pennsylvania for the past 17 years as pastors. She is very involved in overseas missions work as well. She is Co-founder of Captivated for Christ, a ministry that helps former inmates find hope and healing through programming and housing. Angel hopes to cultivate a renewed passion for prayer, spiritual gifts, and inner healing in the body of Christ throughout the nations.